PLANTS
CLOSE UP

Cactus

JOHN AKEROYD

Yew leaf and berries

Pine cone

Peziza vesiculosa
Fungus

Sunflower

PLANTS
CLOSE UP

Mallow

SILVERDALE BOOKS

Produced by
Elm Grove Books Limited
Series Editor Susie Elwes
Consultant Editor
Prof. M. B. Wilkins
Text Editor Colville Wemyss
Angela Wilkes
Art Director Schermuly Design,
Index Hilary Bird
Cover design Steve Flight

Original Edition © 1998
Image Quest Limited
This edition © 2002
Elm Grove Books Limited
Text and photographs in this book
previously published in
Eyewitness 3D Plant

SILVERDALE BOOKS
an imprint of Bookmart Ltd
Registered Number 2372865
Trading as Bookmart Ltd
Desford Road
Enderby
Leicester LE9 5AD

ISBN 1 85605 720-8

A C.I.P. Catalogue record for this title is
available from the British Library.

Printed by Dai Nippon
Printing Company
HongKong

ACKNOWLEDGMENTS
Picture credits
Biofotos Associates 5, 26; Jane Burton 14; Bruce Coleman 7, 17;
J. H. Dickinson 16; Frank Greenaway 6; NHPA 5, 18, 30, 40, 40,
41, 43;
M. B.O Wilkins 9, 13, 28; Kim Taylor 19.

Project Photographers
Tim Hellier,, Justin Peach,
Christopher Parks, Peter Parks

The publishers would also like to thank
Ken Burras, Betty Colville, Alan and Judy Crawford,
Alison Lateria, The Oxford Botanical Gardens
and Time Walker, Abi Peach, Julia Porter,
Richard Tucker, Steven and Sarah Vanderpump,
Arthur and Marion Warland

Stagshorn

CONTENTS

WHAT IS A PLANT?

Plants were one of the first forms of life on Earth and are vital to all life on our planet. They use sunlight to make their food and, in turn, provide a food source for birds, insects, animals, and humans. They also produce oxygen, which all animals need to breathe. Firewood, coal, petroleum, medicines, textiles, and timber all originally come from plants.

KELP SEAWEED
From microscopic plankton to giant sea kelp, algae put more oxygen back into the atmosphere than all the other plants in the world put together.

OAK TREE
Trees are the largest plants. The vast system of narrow tubes running from their roots up to their leaves keeps water and nutrients flowing, sometimes for hundreds of years.

EARTH-STAR FUNGUS
Fungi were traditionally thought of as plants, but are actually distinct from both plants and animals. The earth-star fungus is one of a multitude of different fungi.

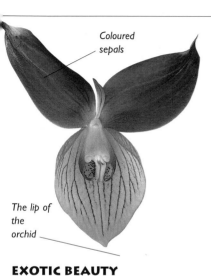

Coloured sepals

The lip of the orchid

EXOTIC BEAUTY
There are about 250,000 different species of flowering plants worldwide. Of these, almost one in twelve are orchids, one of the most attractive and best-known types of flowers.

BUTTERCUP DIMENSION
The roots of most plants occupy a far greater area underground than the stems, leaves and flowers do above the ground.

LICHEN
A lichen is two organisms in one – a fungus teamed with tiny, one-celled algae. They are very tough, and can live almost anywhere.

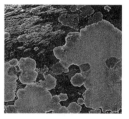

FOSSIL PLANTS
Plants have grown on Earth for hundreds of millions of years. Impressions of some of the earliest plants have been preserved as fossils, formed when the plant decayed in soft earth, leaving behind a mould. This mould was filled by minerals, creating a cast of the original plant.

This fern was growing when dinosaurs roamed the Earth.

GREEN IS THE COLOUR

Leaves are the food factory of a living plant. They come in many different shapes and sizes, but they all contain a green pigment called chlorophyll that absorbs light energy from the sun. This energy is used to make sugar from carbon dioxide in the air and water from the soil. The sugar is the energy source for the whole plant.

SIMPLE LEAVES
Simple leaves have a large, unbroken surface, which enables them to soak up lots of sunlight.

COMPOUND LEAVES
Compound leaves are divided into many small leaf structures.

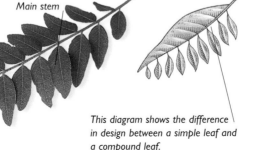

Main stem

This diagram shows the difference in design between a simple leaf and a compound leaf.

HOLEY LEAVES
As a Swiss cheese plant grows, its leaves change from simple leaves to semi-compound leaves.

HORSE CHESTNUT
The leaves of a horse chestnut tree form an umbrella, allowing each leaf to face the sun and absorb light energy. They are arranged in a thin one-leaf-thick canopy; very few leaves overlap each other.

Simple leaves

COLOUR CHANGE
The leaves of many trees are too delicate to survive the cold of winter. In autumn, as the leaves start to die, the green chlorophyll in them breaks down; but their red and yellow pigments (dyes) remain.

A new leaf appears at the top of the tree as the lowest leaf on the stem falls away.

LARCH NEEDLES
Many coniferous trees have stiff, needle-like leaves which resist water-loss and stay green throughout the year.

PALM TREE
The large, compound leaves of this palm grow in a spiral around the trunk, and cannot grow towards the best source of sunlight like the branches of a horse chestnut tree.

Veins protrude on backs of leaves.

Parallel veins are typical of grasses.

UNDER A LEAF

The undersides of most leaves are protected from strong sunlight. Hairs or scales improve this protection. Leaf veins are part of the system that allows water into and out of the leaf. Veins contain two types of cell: xylem cells, which draw water and minerals from the plant's roots to its leaves, and phloem cells, which carry nutrients, produced by photosynthesis, and dissolved in a solution, from the leaves down to the rest of the plant. This process is described as the plant's circulatory system.

GAS VALVES

The surface of a leaf is covered with tiny valves called stomata, which allow gases to pass to and from the leaf and the air. During the day, leaves absorb carbon dioxide from the air and expel oxygen. This process is called photosynthesis. At night they absorb oxygen, to make new cells, and expel the carbon dioxide produced.

THE CYCLE

Photosynthesis uses water, carbon dioxide, and light to produce sugar and oxygen. At night, sugar and oxygen produce new plant cells and release carbon dioxide.

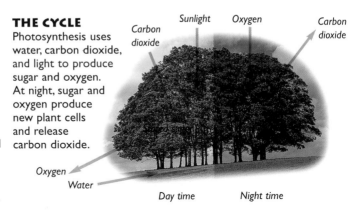

Carbon dioxide

Sunlight

Oxygen

Carbon dioxide

Oxygen

Water

Day time

Night time

The chlorophyll close to the upper surface of the leaf makes it a brighter green.

HIDDEN SUPPORT

Leaf veins are often large and strong. They provide a framework at the back of the leaf to support the large flat leaf surface.

Veins carry fluids in the leaf.

Hollows formed between the veins protect the stomata.

TOP OF THE LEAF

A leaf is covered by a waxy skin called a cuticle. This prevents water loss and protects the leaf cells. The cells near the surface contain the most light absorbing chlorophyll.

Stoma are usually found on the underside of the leaf.

STOMATA

Stomata have sausage-shaped guard cells on either side. These open to take in carbon dioxide or expel oxygen, depending on the time of day. If the plant does not have enough water, the guard cells close the stomata to prevents further moisture loss.

9

FUEL FOR GROWTH

Plants use oxygen in the same way as animals to convert food into energy and new cells. In plants, oxygen breaks down the sugars and carbohydrates produced during photosynthesis in a complex step-by-step process which produces new cells for development and storage. Carbon dioxide and water are released during this process.

Water drop

BEADS OF WATER

The roots of some plants absorb more water than the plant requires. The water is pulled up the plant and is then forced out of small pores around the edges of the leaves in small drops.

The cells circulating fluids in a plant are supported by the surrounding fibrous cells.

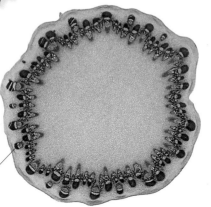

INSIDE A STEM

This cross-section of a plant stem shows its circulatory system for transporting food and water. The circulating system has no moving parts. It consists of two sets of tubes made of different cells: xylem cells, for pulling water and minerals upwards, and phloem cells for circulate sugars around the plant. These are embedded in strong supporting cells.

CANADIAN PONDWEED

Pondweeds live totally submerged in water. Water plants replace oxygen in the water in the same way that land plants replace oxygen in the air. Some of this oxygen dissolves in the water and is used by small underwater animals.

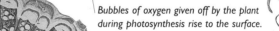
Bubbles of oxygen given off by the plant during photosynthesis rise to the surface.

Leaves of underwater plants need sunlight just like land plants.

Small core of thin walled pith cells

Xylem cells

Outer cortex

New phloem cells continue to be produced.

INSIDE AN OLDER STEM

In this cross-section of a stem, the core consists of pith cells. Xylem cells are arranged radially around this core and show four annual growth rings. Outside these are the Phloem cells contained by the outer cortex.

WHAT'S IN A FLOWER?

Beautiful as flowers are, they are not just for decoration. Every part of a plant has a specific purpose: a flower's purpose is to produce seeds that will grow into new plants. The hypericum flower shown here has the same basic structure as all flowers: female parts (the stigma and ovaries) in the centre, encircled by male parts (the stamens). Around these are rings of petals and sepals, which attract pollinating insects.

CROCUS FLOWERS
The sepals and petals are identical in these flowers. The stamens are often harvested and dried as saffron, which is used to flavour and colour food.

The markings on these petals guide insects towards the nectar in the centre of this mallow flower.

FLOWER PLAN
Colour and scent attract insects to a flower. While they are feeding, they brush pollen onto the projecting stigma and collect pollen from the encircling anthers of the flower.

HYPERICUM **PERFECTION**

The hypericum flower shows the three of the four concentric rings of specialized leaves that make up the petals, stamens, and ovaries of a typical flower. The fourth ring of sepals is underneath the petals; it is visible in a cross-section.

A CROSS-SECTION

This flower is arranged in four concentric rings. The ovaries are fused in the centre of the flower. When pollen fertilizes the ovaries, they start the process of seed production.

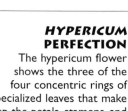

Each anther produces pollen in four pollen sacs.

The ovaries share a stalk bearing the stigma at the top.

The stigma stands above the anthers, its sticky surface ready to collect pollen from insects as they arrive at the flower.

Each hypericum flower sits between two leaves.

Style

Stigma

Ovary

Anther

Filament

Stamen

Petal

Sepal

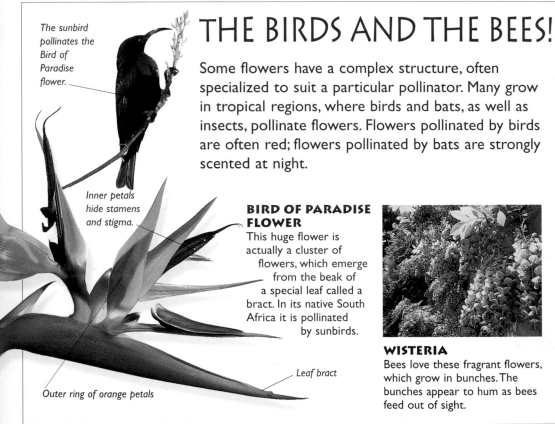

The sunbird pollinates the Bird of Paradise flower.

THE BIRDS AND THE BEES!

Some flowers have a complex structure, often specialized to suit a particular pollinator. Many grow in tropical regions, where birds and bats, as well as insects, pollinate flowers. Flowers pollinated by birds are often red; flowers pollinated by bats are strongly scented at night.

Inner petals hide stamens and stigma.

BIRD OF PARADISE FLOWER

This huge flower is actually a cluster of flowers, which emerge from the beak of a special leaf called a bract. In its native South Africa it is pollinated by sunbirds.

WISTERIA

Bees love these fragrant flowers, which grow in bunches. The bunches appear to hum as bees feed out of sight.

Leaf bract

Outer ring of orange petals

PASSION FLOWER

Missionaries used this tropical flower to illustrate Christ's Crucifixion: ten petals for the apostles (leaving out Judas and St.Peter), the corona for the crown of thorns, five stamen for the wounds and three stigmas for the nails. The five stamens are arranged on a tree.

A ring of hair-like outgrowths from the base of the petals forms the distinctive corona.

Stigma

Stamen

Anther

Filament

Sepal

The whole head of the flower turns and follows the sun's path during the day

When a bee lands, its weight opens the flower.

SUNFLOWER

The flowers of the daisy family, such as the sunflower, are either flat or have domed clusters of tiny florets.

SNAPDRAGON

The anthers and stigmas are hidden deep inside a snapdragon flower. A bee must land on the petal platform to open the flower so it can crawl inside. While it gorges on the nectar, it collects and transfers pollen.

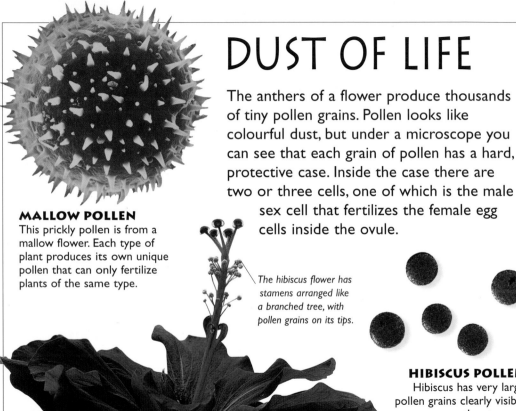

MALLOW POLLEN
This prickly pollen is from a mallow flower. Each type of plant produces its own unique pollen that can only fertilize plants of the same type.

DUST OF LIFE

The anthers of a flower produce thousands of tiny pollen grains. Pollen looks like colourful dust, but under a microscope you can see that each grain of pollen has a hard, protective case. Inside the case there are two or three cells, one of which is the male sex cell that fertilizes the female egg cells inside the ovule.

The hibiscus flower has stamens arranged like a branched tree, with pollen grains on its tips.

HIBISCUS POLLEN
Hibiscus has very large pollen grains clearly visible on the stamens.

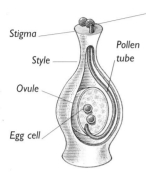

Stigma

Style

Pollen tube

Ovule

Egg cell

Pollen grains are collected on the flower's stigma.

POLLEN PATH
After pollen has landed on a stigma, it grows a fine tube down the style towards the ovules. Each grain of pollen can fertilize a single ovule.

Stigma

Lily flowers are frequently spotted, highly scented, and brightly coloured.

POLLEN EXPOSED
Lily pollen is produced in the anthers well below the stigma to prevent the pollen produced by the flower from fertilizing its own ovules.

Grains of pollen are visible on the anthers.

The visiting insects collect the lily's own pollen from the anthers.

LILY STIGMA
Lily pollen is visible and easily distributed by insects as they fly from lily flower to lily flower. If it is brushed off lily pollen will stain hands and clothes, it is difficult to remove.

The filament holds the anther forward, clear of the stigma.

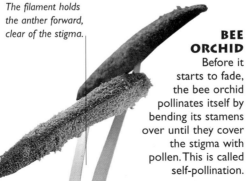

BEE ORCHID
Before it starts to fade, the bee orchid pollinates itself by bending its stamens over until they cover the stigma with pollen. This is called self-pollination.

DIFFERENT SCENTS

Many flowers are sweetly scented, to lure pollinating insects into them in search of nectar. Some flowers, however, have a disgusting smell, to attract midges that normally feed on dung. Flowers release their scent at different times, depending on whether they are pollinated by day-time or night-time creatures.

BIRD POLLINATION

Several flowers are pollinated by birds that are attracted by their colour, especially red, and the scent of nectar, which they eat. As the bird feeds, pollen grains stick to its feathers and are unwittingly carried to the next flower that the bird visits.

A butterfly unrolls its long tongue to reach the nectar.

INSECT POLLINATION

Insects are attracted to flowers by their colour, and by the nectar and pollen, which they eat. Flowers secrete nectar, a sugary liquid, from special glands called nectaries.

Leaflike sheath.

**1** Midge enters lily past stiff hairs which hang down to prevent it leaving before anthers shed their pollen.

**2** Male flowers remain closed as midge enters.

**3** Pollen from midge is brushed off onto female flowers.

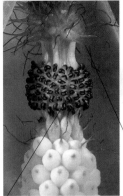

**4** Male flowers open and shed pollen onto captive midges.

Small flowers which grow on the column give off a horrid smell.

THE ARUM FLOWER

The arum flower consists of a column or spadix protected by a leaf-like sheath. The pollinators are lured into the flower by its nasty smell.

**5** Hairs at the top wither, and midges are free to carry this pollen away.

INSECT POLLINATION

Many insects tend to feed on the same plants, carrying pollen between different plants of the same type.

INSECTS AND POLLEN

Pollen grains often have a sticky surface that sticks to a bee's furry body. Bees comb pollen from their bodies and carry it back to the hive.

BLOWING IN THE WIND

A sharp spike of male flowers at the top of the bulrush catches the wind. Below, the female flowers are packed in a sausage-shaped cluster ready to receive pollen from other bulrushes.

Grasses, sedges and rushes, docks and plantains, and many types of tree all rely on the wind to carry pollen between them for fertilization. The flowers of these plants are usually green with long, flexible filaments and feathery stigmas to catch some of the vast amounts of pollen borne along by the wind.

Styles

BULRUSH
Bulrushes grow in water and are a familiar sight in lakes, streams, and ponds. In the past the long reeds were used as floor coverings, which could be thrown away when dirty.

LARCH CONES
Pines and other conifers have male and female cones instead of flowers. The female pine cone has wooden scales arranged in a spiral. Each scale has two ovules on its surface. Male cones drop off after shedding pollen.

MAIZE

Maize, or sweet corn, is usually planted in large numbers so that the wind can swirl the pollen around the crop.

Maize pollen fills the air with each gust of wind. This pollen has a smooth, non-sticky surface to allow it move easily on air currents.

POLLEN STORM

This enlarged view of maize catkins clearly shows they are made up of masses of tiny male flowers. These flowers grow at the top of the maize stem. In this position the fine, light grains of pollen are easily swept into the air by the wind and carried to neighbouring plants.

Female oak flowers on the tip of a branch collect pollen from the wind.

Catkins of male flowers appear before the tiny female flowers open.

OAK

Oak trees flower in summer. Male flowers grow in catkins that fall off when they have released pollen.

HAZEL

Hazel produces male catkins and small female flowers in autumn. The wind pollinates the plants after the leaves have fallen.

FROM FLOWER TO FRUIT

A poppy flower is pollinated by insects leaving pollen from other poppies on its stigmas. The pollen germinates and a male cell passes down a tube called the style, to fertilize a female cell in an ovule. Each fertilized ovule becomes a seed and the ovary that surrounds it develops into a fruit.

The flower is crumpled into the bud.

THE FLOWER
The fully opened flower reveals the rings of petals, the male stamens, and in the centre the fused female parts of the flower. These are the stigma, style, ovary, and ovules, which are collectively called the carpel.

THE BUD
At first the flower is a compact bud enclosed by protective green sepals. The petals grow tightly and fold symmetrically around the other developing flower parts.

Bright colour attracts insect pollinators.

The carpel

POPPY CENTRE
The poppy stigmas are fused together into one circular, yellow disc in the centre of the flower for collecting pollen.

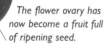

The flower ovary has now become a fruit full of ripening seed.

Withered stamens

TRANSFORMATION
The stamens droop and fall away as the seed capsule swells and the seeds form inside. The seed capsule develops from the ovary of the poppy flower into a hard green fruit.

POPPY SHAKER
As the poppy fruit ripens, it acts like a seed shaker. Every time the wind blows, the seed head sways and shakes out some seeds. Seeds are distributed in all directions around the adult plant.

FRUIT AND SEEDS
The seed capsule is the fruit of the poppy. It remains after it has scattered its seeds. Other fruits, such as burrs, carry their seed away, while some fruits are eaten by animals before their seed is expelled.

Poppy seeds

SEEDS OF LIFE

The grains of wheat fall when the whole ear ripens.

A ripe seed consists of an embryo, that is a very young plant complete with a root, a shoot, and leaves, as well as its own store of food. The food store provides energy for the embryo to start growing. In flowering plants, the seeds are encased in protective fruits. These come in a great variety of forms and may be dry and hard, or fleshy and soft when ripe.

WHEAT
Each wheat seed is really a fruit and contains large stores of starch and protein, ready for the seed to use as it starts growing.

APPLE
The seeds of an apple lie deep inside the fruit. The apple grows from part of the flower. If an animal eats apple seeds, they pass through its digestive system and are dispersed in the animal's dung.

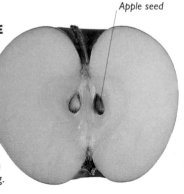

Apple seed

24

PEA PODS

The pods of peas and beans are their fruits. As a pod ripens, it dries out and splits along the edge to release its seeds.

Sprouting shoot

STRAWBERRY FRUITS

The strawberry is called a 'false fruit'. The red flesh is formed from the base of the flower, the receptacle, not from the female flower parts. Each single seed is actually a whole fruit, with a visibly developing shoot sunk into the flesh.

Strawberry plant

BANANA BERRIES!

A banana is an elongated berry, a fleshy fruit with many seeds. The fruit hangs in huge leaf-like bracts that contain many individual bananas.

Young bananas

HIDDEN FRUITS

Strawberries grow beneath a strawberry plant's leaves. When ripe, their bright colour attracts feeding birds that disperse the fruits in their droppings.

PLANTS AND PARACHUTES

When seeds are ripe, they are shed from the plant. Many of them simply fall to the ground and take root nearby. The seeds and fruits of some plants, however, have wings, plumes, hooks, or spines to help them travel as far as possible. They are carried by water, wind, and by animals.

The scales open during dry weather to drop seeds.

LARCH CONES

When a larch cone is ripe, the scales open to release the winged seeds, which can float a short distance in the wind. Seeds that fall directly under the tree rarely survive because the sunlight is blocked out by the mature tree.

Two pine seeds attached to a single scale.

The coconut inside its husk has begun to sprout.

COCONUT

These huge fruits with their fibrous husks are buoyant and can float thousands of miles on ocean currents.

SYCAMORE

The wings of a sycamore seed are shaped like propeller blades. The seeds whirl a short distance from the adult tree and can even take root in a crack in a wall.

Flying seed

Each floret of a dandelion flower produces a single seed with its own feathery parachute.

DANDELION CLOCK

Dandelion seeds are attached to small pits in the flower head. Each seed has a stalk with a circle of fine hairs at the end which will hoist it into the wind. This parachute structure allows the seed to travel long distances in light winds.

WOOD AVENS

These burrs are the fruits of wood avens. Numerous hooks attach them firmly to animal fur and wool. The burs ride on the animal until they either fall or are pulled off. The seeds inside a bur develop into plants.

DANDELION

A dandelion seed head is an excellent launching pad for long-distance travel. When the seeds are ripe, the cells attaching them to the seed head shrivel. The silken parachutes are then lifted into the air by the first passing breeze and can be carried for miles.

GRAIN OF CORN

This seed has been cut in half and its starch-rich food store has been stained black. The root, shoot, and first leaves of the embryo are all visible.

READY, STEADY, GROW!

A seed is a tiny dormant plant with its own food store. The seed uses the food store to grow until it can start to make its own food. In peas and beans, the food is stored in the seed leaves. When moisture, light, and heat are suitable, the seed begins to grow, or germinate. Guided by gravity, the root pushes through the seed coat down into the ground. The shoot then unfurls and grows towards the sunlight.

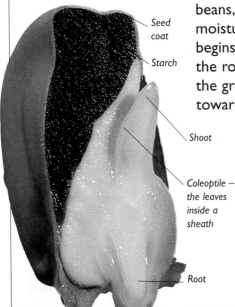

Seed coat

Starch

Shoot

Coleoptile – the leaves inside a sheath

Root

PEA GERMINATION

This pea seed takes 17 days to germinate.

1 The seed absorbs water and starts to grow immediately.

Scar where it was attached to the pod.

A shoot unfolds from this bump.

2 The root pushes out first and grows rapidly.

QUICK START

When water enters the seed, germination begins. The primary root of this bean seed emerges within 48 hours.

Bean seed do not germinate immediately. However, some seeds, such as willow tree seeds, can only germinate within one week of their formation.

Seed leaves containing stored food

The root emerges first.

A tiny shoot with folded leaves opens out between the two seed leaves.

Foliage leaves

Leaf bud

3 The root grows longer and the delicate shoot emerges from between the seed leaves.

Shoot

The pea remains underground as the shoot appears through the soil.

Root

4 The shoot lengthens to carry the foliage leaves above the soil. The seed leaves remain below the ground.

5 The seed has completed all the stages of germination. Its root and shoot continue to lengthen as the seed leaves shrink.

The root begins to branch and spread out.

SEEDLESS PLANTS

Some plants do not flower or bear seeds in order to reproduce. Instead, they reproduce by means of tiny spores that lack a seed coat or food store. There are four groups of non-flowering plants: algae, including most water plants, mosses and liverworts, ferns and horsetails, and fungi.

Puffball spores are so fine they look like smoke as they rise into the air.

PUFFBALL
Raindrops hitting the papery skin of a puffball fungus cause a cloud of dust-like spores to explode from its round cap. Fungi feed on dead or living plant or animal tissue.

WRACK
This giant seaweed reproduces by spores set adrift in the water. It grows in masses on rocky seashores.

Liverworts are low-growing plants without true stems, leaves, or roots.

The polypody fern in its sporophyte form produces spores on the underside of its leaves. When the spores are ripe, they are thrown into the air.

LIVERWORT CUP
Some liverworts need water for reproduction. Gemmae form in special cups on the surface of the plant, and germinate without fertilization. Rain splashes the gemmae out to grow into a new plant.

Round, green gemmae look like tiny bird's eggs in a nest. They germinate into a new liverwort plant.

FERN FORMS LARGE AND SMALL
Land ferns have two forms: sporophytes that produce spores that germinate and develop into small, short-lived gametophytes.

Gametophytes produce gametes, or sex cells, from which a new sporophyte develops.

ON THE MOVE

Plants do not just grow but also move in response to sunlight, warmth, or even touch. Some flowers turn to face the sun or close their petals at night. Climbers twine themselves around a support. Other plants, such as those that trap insects, react so quickly you can see them moving.

CLIMBING SUPPORT

The stems of some climbing plants twist themselves around other plants or uprights for support. Other plants have tendrils that twine around anything they touch.

REACHING THE LIGHT

Beneath the soil, a shoot grows rapidly towards the surface. On reaching sunlight its stem straightens and growth slows.

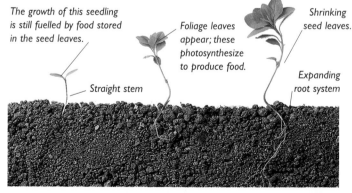

The growth of this seedling is still fuelled by food stored in the seed leaves.

Foliage leaves appear; these photosynthesize to produce food.

Shrinking seed leaves.

Straight stem

Expanding root system

The signal to start flowering is given by a chemical message within the plant. At first the petals are curled around each other, like a tightly furled umbrella.

The petals expand but do not open completely.

CYCLAMEN FLOWERS

Cyclamen reproduce only from seeds since their corms do not divide or reproduce at all. It is vital for their fully opened flowers to display all their reproductive parts.

Stigma and stamens are exposed when insect pollinators are most active. Flowering plants produce flowers at the same time each year. Their biological clocks are set by the length of the hours of darkness between dusk and dawn.

SUNFLOWER

Most varieties of sunflower have a large central disc made up of hundreds of tiny individual flowers packed closely together. If you watch a field of sunflowers, you will see that they always face the sun as it moves through the day.

SILVER BIRCH
The bark of a
silver birch splits
horizontally
around the
growing tree
trunk to allow for
further growth.
The bark protects
the trunk and
prevents
water loss.

*The bark consists
of dead cells
impregnated with
a waterproof
substance.*

*Bark is replenished
from within by a
layer of new cells.*

A TREE IS FOR LIFE

Most trees are large flowering plants that can
live for many years. They need to be both
strong and able to draw water up to the highest
branches from deep below the soil. Water
moves through pipe-like chains of woody cells
that strengthen the tree's trunk and branches.
Outward growth occurs in cells beneath the
tree's bark.

BRANCHES
When a tree grows a
new branch, the water-
conducting cells must
supply water to the
leaves and shoots on
the branch. To carry
the great weight of
a branch, plant cells
grow more thickly
on its underside where
the branch meets
the main trunk.

*Heartwood provides
support and stores waste.*

*Sapwood contains
the fluid transport
system.*

*Openings in the
bark of older
trees allow gases
to move in
and out.*

Each acorn contains one oak seed.

This seedling may grow into a tree. It is rooted in fertile leaf litter but sunlight is filtered by the leaf canopy and it may not have room to spread out.

Sapwood is made up of the water-carrying xylem cells.

OAK GROWTH

Many acorns sprout from the woodland floor. Most are eaten as small, tender shoots. Lack of sunlight slows the growth of small trees. In the open, a mature tree grows a huge dome of leaves.

TREE RINGS

Tree rings are visible when the tree is cut. They show each year's growth of water-carrying cells within the trunk. Each ring has two parts: soft spring wood and hard summer wood.

Dark heartwood at the centre is the oldest part of a tree trunk. The cells here no longer carry water.

Outer waterproof leaves

The new plant grows from the top of the bulb.

Shrivelled roots from previous year

WINTER STORES

Annual plants grow, develop seeds, and die in a single year. Biennial plants follow a two-year cycle. Perennial plants live for several years, and must store food to use when it is too dark to photosynthesize. These plants usually keep their food underground, away from animals, fierce summer heat, or winter frost. Many plants can reproduce from these food stores.

INSIDE AN ONION

An onion is a resting bud surrounded and protected by fleshy food-storing leaves called scale leaves. Scale leaves often form buds, which can develop into separate plants.

STRAWBERRY RUNNERS

A strawberry plant produces long stems called stolons. Roots and buds form at intervals on the stolon.

New strawberry plants grow from a stolon root.

Developing stolon root

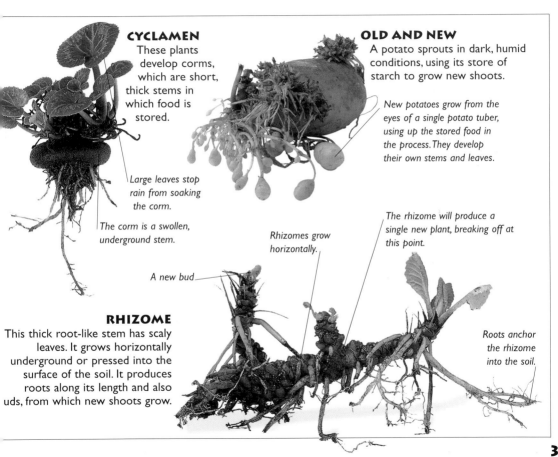

CYCLAMEN
These plants develop corms, which are short, thick stems in which food is stored.

Large leaves stop rain from soaking the corm.

The corm is a swollen, underground stem.

A new bud

OLD AND NEW
A potato sprouts in dark, humid conditions, using its store of starch to grow new shoots.

New potatoes grow from the eyes of a single potato tuber, using up the stored food in the process. They develop their own stems and leaves.

The rhizome will produce a single new plant, breaking off at this point.

Rhizomes grow horizontally.

RHIZOME
This thick root-like stem has scaly leaves. It grows horizontally underground or pressed into the surface of the soil. It produces roots along its length and also uds, from which new shoots grow.

Roots anchor the rhizome into the soil.

MEAT EATERS!

Amazingly, some plants eat meat. These plants grow in places that are short of nutrients, such as in peat bogs or on rainforest trees, and specialize in attracting and trapping insects. The insects provide the plants with the nitrogen they need for normal growth. An exploring insect cannot escape once the trap is sprung. Fluids from the plant slowly dissolve and digest the insect's body.

Fly trapped by sticky hairs.

SUNDEW
These small plants grow on moorland and flower in summer.

Tiny glands contain digestive fluids. Each leaf can only trap once.

BLADDERWORT
Bladderworts grow in boggy pools. Triggered by sensitive hairs, the plants suck tiny creatures into their fluid-filled bladders.

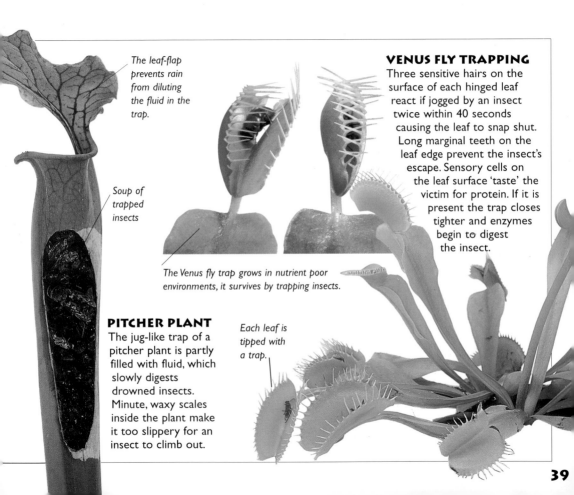

The leaf-flap prevents rain from diluting the fluid in the trap.

Soup of trapped insects

VENUS FLY TRAPPING

Three sensitive hairs on the surface of each hinged leaf react if jogged by an insect twice within 40 seconds causing the leaf to snap shut. Long marginal teeth on the leaf edge prevent the insect's escape. Sensory cells on the leaf surface 'taste' the victim for protein. If it is present the trap closes tighter and enzymes begin to digest the insect.

The Venus fly trap grows in nutrient poor environments, it survives by trapping insects.

PITCHER PLANT

The jug-like trap of a pitcher plant is partly filled with fluid, which slowly digests drowned insects. Minute, waxy scales inside the plant make it too slippery for an insect to climb out.

Each leaf is tipped with a trap.

LIVING TOGETHER

Not all plants manufacture green chlorophyll to produce their own food. Some plants, called saprophytes, absorb nutrition from decomposing matter. Other plants, called parasites, depend on other living plants. Lichens are formed by a fungus but are dependent for food upon an algae partner. Plants that exist together and benefit from each other are said to live symbiotically.

DODDER
This parasite twines over other plants, sucking out the food and water.

BIRD'S-NEST ORCHID
The saprophytic bird's-nest orchid has yellowish-brown flowers. Fungi in its roots pull the nutrients it requires from decaying leaves.

OLD LICHEN
Lichens grow slowly and can live over 4,000 years. They survive in extreme conditions, including both hot and cold deserts. In the Arctic they are an important food source.

This cup-shaped tip holds reproductive spores.

In close-up, this lichen looks like an ancient forest. The upright growth belongs to the fungus. The lichen's colour comes from photosynthesizing green algae embedded in the fungus.

RAFFLESIA
The largest flower in the world belongs to this parasitic plant, which lives on the roots of vines in the rainforests of Southeast Asia.

Mistletoe invades the water and mineral supply which its host plant has drawn from the soil.

MISTLETOE
A partial parasite, mistletoe grows on trees. It can photosynthesize in its green leaves. However, all its water and minerals are absorbed from its host plant.

This vast flower attracts flies with its unpleasant, rotten smell.

Root-like structures penetrate the bark of the host tree.

RISING DAMP

Mosses and ferns do not flower but reproduce by spores. A spore germinates to give rise to a tiny plant with both male and female sexual organs. The male cells (gametes) need water so they can swim to and fertilize the female egg cells. Mosses and some ferns grow in damp places where they can reproduce successfully.

A tree fern carries all its fronds right at the top of its thick stem.

TREE FERN

Ferns range in size from tiny, moss-like plants to trees as high as 20m (65ft), with massive trunks and palm-like fronds.

FERN FROND

The leaf-like fern frond is curled over tightly to protect the delicate young growth inside. It slowly unfurls as it matures.

MOSSY CARPET

A thick mat of green leaves supports the brown spore capsules. Mosses have neither flowers nor roots, so they grow in damp places where each cell can absorb the required water and minerals.

Masses of spores explode in a visible cloud.

MASSES OF MOSS

Moss has no system for moving water within itself. Each cell absorbs water and minerals from its surroundings.

Moss leaves lack a protective outer layer to stop water loss.

TWO PLANTS IN ONE

Moss spores grow into leafy plants that produce free-swimming male sperm cells and egg cells. A fertilized egg grows into a different plant, with a stem and spore head, on top of the first plant. The spores it produces germinate into plants.

A SPORE LIFE

Fungi were once thought to be plants, but scientists now believe they form a separate kingdom from either plants or animals. Many fungi live on decaying organic matter, although some depend on other plants for their nutrients. All reproduce by shedding huge quantities of minute spores.

DUNG FUNGI

These small fungi absorb nutrients from animal dung. Without fungi speeding up the process of breaking down organic matter, the world would be full of waste material!

Dung fungi send microscopic threads into the dung.

ORANGE-PEEL FUNGUS

This is one of the many species of brightly coloured cup fungi that only grow in spring and autumn.

Bright colours are a warning that these fungi may be poisonous. However, not all poisonous fungi are coloured!

HONEYCOMB?

The honeycomb is the fruiting body of this fungus. It extends long strands of mycelium into the tree, which it slowly absorbs.

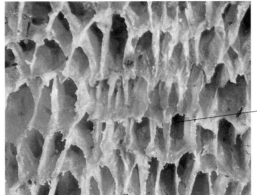

Reproductive spores are formed in special cells. When spores are shed, a honeycomb is left, which is a hunting ground for insects.

BRACKET FUNGUS

The bracket fungus is one of the many varieties that grows on trees. It sticks out from the tree trunk in a series of small shelves.

FLY AGARIC

This toadstool has a ring at the base of its stem. It sheds spores from gills underneath the cap. It is very poisonous.

A red cap warns animals not to touch this toadstool.

BLUE MOULD

Blue moulds on food are tiny fungi.

Mould spores are visible as blue dust.

Small kelp fronds

WATER PLANTS

Underwater plants are almost all algae. They range from huge kelps and seaweeds to numerous single-celled structures. The single-celled plants, such as the volvox, sometimes form colonies. The volume of algae in the sea is immense and the balance of oxygen in the atmosphere depends on their continual photosynthesis. With few exceptions, flowering plants live only in fresh water.

KELP
This familiar seaweed grows long fronds, which wave in an underwater forest. Brown kelp fixes itself to rocks. Other types float freely like vast blankets.

MANGROVES
These tropical trees grow in salt marshes and help stop the erosion of coastlines. The stilt-like roots trap mud as it is washed into the sea and anchor the trees firmly against the forces of the tides and waves.

VOLVOX

Volvox live in fresh water. They are formed from thousands of single-celled algae, which link together into tiny ball-shaped colonies. Their green outline shows the many chloroplast cells they contain. These cells photosynthesize food, using energy absorbed from sunlight, which is why the volvox lives near the surface of the water.

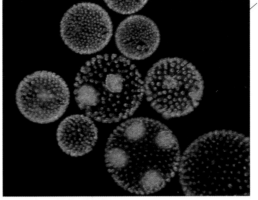

Small, new volvox, called daughter cells, are formed, by cell division inside the adult volvox.

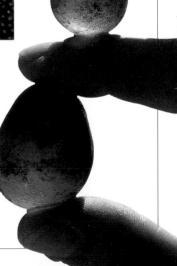

WATER LILY

Water lilies flower in summer when insect pollinators are active. They are attached to the bed of a pond or lake by their long, tough roots. Their floating leaves shelter all kinds of underwater creatures.

Flowers appear above the water to attract pollinating insects.

ALGAL "EGGS"

In warm, tropical waters, single alga grown into an egg-like form. These are the largest single celled plants that are known.

WATER STORES

Plants that live in deserts are adapted to store water in their thick, fleshy leaves and stems; they are called succulents. In some succulents, photosynthesis takes place in the stem, as the leaves have developed into sharp spines to protect them from grazing animals.

HOUSE LEEKS
The house leek's succulent evergreen leaves store water in specialized leaf cells. This plant has clusters of star-shaped flowers in summer.

Fat green leaves of Frithia pulchra *store water.*

CACTI
Cacti range in size and shape from small, round, spiky balls to huge, tree-like plants up to 20m (65ft) tall. Not all cacti have spines.

GREEN FINGERS
The fleshy leaves of these succulents look like fingers with blunt, flattened tips.

ECHINOCERUS

The coloured flower of the Echinocerus cactus rises above its sharp spikes so that insects can pollinate it without injury. There are 16 white spikes in a ring surrounding each thick, dark, central spike.

SUCCULENT TREE

This *Aloe ferox* belongs to a family of small, evergreen trees, shrubs, and climbers. Spines edge its fleshy leaves.

These euphorbia spines are on vertical ridges.

Anthers brush pollen onto visiting insects.

Cacti have spines and hairs arranged in rings.

EUPHORBIA

Some euphorbias have sharp spines; all have a milky sap that causes irritation on contact with the skin.

SHARP PLANTS

Plants have evolved an elaborate system of physical and chemical defences to protect themselves from grazing mammals and insect predators. The most obvious defences are spines and thorns. Stinging hairs penetrate skin, but the stinging, irritation, and pain are caused by the chemicals they release. These special defences are usually modified from stems, branches, leaves, or hairs.

SPANISH BAYONET
This variety of yucca plant has razor-sharp, sword-shaped leaves to deter grazers.

CROWN OF THORNS
The tough thorns of this tropical plant protects its young shoots and seed pods from grazing animals, which might be tempted to eat it when other food is scarce.

Thorns grow out of the main stem.

STINGING NETTLE

These plants attract all sorts of butterflies and moths. They are considered a weed by gardeners.

Each fine hair is loaded with formic acid and histamines. They are set at different angles to pierce in all directions at once.

Head is made up of many tiny flowers.

Tiny yellow flowers are hidden by red petal-like leaves.

In close-up, you can see that each fragile nettle hair has a round tip. A light touch snaps the hair, leaving a sharp edge to pierce the skin. The hair is filled with a cocktail of chemicals that flow into the tiny wound, causing immediate pain.

ROSE

The rose's sharp, hooked horns pierce and tear the skin of mammals. The thorns also enable wild roses to clamber over other plants.

THISTLE

Thistles are often spiny all over, but the sharpest spines surround the flower head.

POISON!

Some plants produce a range of poisonous chemicals that deter insects, grazing animals, and fungi from eating them. But these same chemicals have been used since prehistoric times to cure fever, infection, and sickness. Chemists continue to develop life-saving medicines from plant-produced chemicals, including poisons.

YEW

Nearly every part of the slow-growing yew is poisonous. However, new drugs have been developed from yew, which have been used effectively against some cancers.

MAPLE TREE

Sap from the sugar maple was first eaten by Native Americans. It nourished the weak during winter.

DRUGS FOR HEARTS

Foxgloves naturally produce digitalis, a drug used to slow the heart rate. Some species are grown commercially to manufacture heart medicine. The flowers are poisonous.

Bumblebees force their fat bodies inside these flowers to reach the nectar.

POISON IVY

If poison ivy leaves are bruised, a minute quantity of milky yellow sap leaks out. This causes itching and blisters on the skin.

Ivy stem can twist itself around a tree trunk.

Poison ivy is often covered by leaves of other plants and can be difficult to see.

The cinnabar moth caterpillar eats the poisonous leaves of the ragwort.

DEADLY NIGHTSHADE

The drug atropine is extracted from this very poisonous relative of the potato.

Deadly nightshade is used in an eye drop to expand the pupil during eye examinations.

RAGWORT

All ragworts are poisonous. The cinnabar moth caterpillar feeds on the leaves to make itself poisonous too. Its coloured stripes act as a warning to hungry birds.

Blackberry

INDEX

Bryony

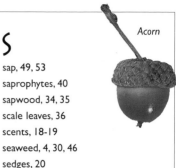

Acorn

Horse chestnut leaf